Jesus Listens

FOR
Advent & Christmas

PRAYERS FOR THE SEASON

Sarah Young

THOMAS NELSON
Since 1798

Dear Reader,

As we celebrate the birth of Jesus and anticipate His coming, my hope is that this book will help you approach Him confidently and joyfully in prayer—finding peaceful rest in His Presence.

It's such a blessing to know that Jesus listens to every one of our prayers! Whether our Christmas season is busy and stressful, wonderfully joyous, sad and lonely, or a combination of all of them, Jesus wants us to come to Him with everything. He invites us to share our burdens with Him and to sit at His feet and rejoice over His coming. He loves us perfectly and is constantly caring for us, whether we're aware of His Presence with us or not.

Whatever our needs are, we can take everything to Jesus—our struggles and confusion, our prayers and petitions, our thanksgiving and praise. After pouring out our hearts to Him, we can ask Him to fill us with His wondrous peace. To receive this glorious gift, we need to relax in Jesus' Presence and *trust Him wholeheartedly*—instead of *relying on our own understanding* (Proverbs 3:5 NET).

I consider it a wonderful privilege and responsibility to pray for readers of my books, and I make this a top priority each morning. I've found that no matter how I feel when I first get out of bed, I feel better and stronger after spending this precious time with Jesus. And you readers can start your day feeling encouraged because you know I'm praying for you!

Sometimes when I'm feeling stressed or overwhelmed, I sit quietly and breathe slowly while praying, "Jesus, help me relax in Your peace." If I continue praying this way for a few moments, I invariably relax and feel calmer.

This Advent and Christmas, I hope you will enjoy the peaceful presence of our Savior. As you read the prayers in this book, I encourage you to make them your own—using them to guide you as you express your heartfelt longings to the Lord. May you have a blessed Christmas of prayer!

Remember that I will be praying for you. Most importantly, remember that Jesus is Immanuel, *God with us*—and He is with you, listening to all your prayers.

Bountiful blessings!

Sarah Young

GRACIOUS GOD,

The Bible promises that *those who wait for You will gain new strength*. I love to spend time waiting in Your Presence, even though multitasking and staying busy have become the norm. During the Advent season, there are *more* things to do than usual. Please help me break free for a while from all the activity and demands. As I *seek Your Face* and enjoy Your Presence, I ponder the essential truth that Christmas is all about *You*.

Waiting with You is an act of faith—trusting that prayer really does make a difference. So I *come to You with my weariness and burdens*, being candidly real with You. While I rest in Your Presence and tell You about my concerns, You lift heavy burdens from my aching shoulders. I'm grateful that *You are able to do immeasurably more than all I ask or imagine*!

As I arise from these quiet moments with You, I delight in hearing You whisper, "I am with you." And I rejoice in the *new strength* gained through spending time with You.

IN YOUR ENERGIZING NAME, JESUS, AMEN

Rest in Me, My child,
forgetting about
the worries of the
world. Focus on Me—
Immanuel—and let
My living Presence
envelop you in Peace.

Those who wait for the L<small>ORD</small> will gain new strength; they will mount up with wings like eagles, they will run and not get tired, they will walk and not become weary.

I<small>SAIAH</small> 40:31 <small>NASB</small>

"Come to me, all you who are weary and burdened, and I will give you rest."

M<small>ATTHEW</small> 11:28

Now to him who is able to do immeasurably more than all we ask or imagine, according to his power that is at work within us.

E<small>PHESIANS</small> 3:20

My delightful Lord,

This is the day that You have made! As I rejoice in this day of life, it will yield precious gifts and beneficial training. I want to walk with You along the high road of thanksgiving—discovering all the delights You have prepared for me.

To protect my thankfulness throughout this holiday season, I need to remember that I reside in a fallen world where blessings and sorrows intermingle freely. When I'm too focused on troubles, I walk through a day that's brimming with beauty and brightness while seeing only the grayness of my thoughts. Neglecting the practice of giving thanks darkens my mind and dims my vision.

Lord, please clear up my vision by helping me remember to thank You at all times. When I'm grateful, I can walk through the darkest days with Joy in my heart because I know that *the Light of Your Presence* is still shining on me. So *I rejoice in You*—my delightful, steadfast Companion.

In Your bright, shining Name, Jesus, amen

When you approach
Me with thanksgiving,
the Light of My
Presence pours into
you, transforming you
through and through.

This is the day that the Lord has made;
let us rejoice and be glad in it.

Psalm 118:24 ESV

Devote yourselves to prayer, being
watchful and thankful.

Colossians 4:2

Blessed are those who have learned to acclaim
you, who walk in the light of your presence,
O Lord. They rejoice in your name all day
long; they exult in your righteousness.

Psalm 89:15–16

ALL-KNOWING GOD,

This is a wonderful time of year, but it can also be an exhausting time for me. *When my spirit grows faint within me, it is You who know my way.* This is one of the benefits of weakness; it highlights the reality that I cannot find my way without Your guidance. Whenever I'm feeling weary or confused, I can choose to look away from these feelings and turn wholeheartedly toward You. As I pour out my heart to You, I find rest in the Presence of the One who knows my way perfectly—all the way to heaven.

Help me to continue this practice of gazing at You even during the times when I'm feeling confident and strong. This is when I am most at risk of going in the wrong direction. Instead of assuming that I know the next step of my journey, I'm learning to make my plans in Your Presence—asking You to guide me.

Please remind me often that *Your ways and thoughts are higher than mine, as the heavens are higher than the earth.* Remembering this great truth draws me into worshiping You, *the High and Lofty One who inhabits eternity.* I rejoice that even though *You dwell in the high and holy place,* You reach down to show me the way I should go.

IN YOUR EXALTED NAME, JESUS, AMEN

Trust Me with every
fiber of your being!
What I can accomplish
in and through
you is proportional
to how much you
depend on Me.

When my spirit grows faint within me,
it is you who know my way.

PSALM 142:3

"As the heavens are higher than the earth,
so are my ways higher than your ways and
my thoughts than your thoughts."

ISAIAH 55:9

Thus says the High and Lofty One who inhabits
eternity, whose name is Holy: "I dwell in the high
and holy place, with him who has a contrite and
humble spirit, to revive the spirit of the humble,
and to revive the heart of the contrite ones."

ISAIAH 57:15 NKJV

MY LOVING LORD,

In the midst of this busy season, You continually invite me to draw near. I love to hear You whispering in my heart: "Come to Me, beloved. *I have loved you with an everlasting Love. I have drawn you with lovingkindness.*" I respond to Your beautiful invitation by being still in Your Presence— relaxing and *fixing my thoughts on You.* And I meditate on the glorious truth that *You are continually with me.* This rock-solid reality provides a firm foundation for my life.

The world I inhabit is constantly in flux—I can find no solid ground here. So I desperately need to stay aware of *You* as I go about my day. I know I won't be able to do this perfectly, but I can return to You time after time, praying: "Jesus, keep me aware of Your loving Presence." I like to let this prayer continually echo in my heart and mind—drawing me back to You when my thoughts start to wander away.

I've found that the more of You I have in my life through living close to You, the more joyful I am. This blesses not only me but others—as Your Joy flows through me to them.

IN YOUR BLESSED NAME, JESUS, AMEN

A person who is open to My Presence is exceedingly precious to Me.

The LORD has appeared of old to me, saying:
"Yes, I have loved you with an everlasting love;
therefore with lovingkindness I have drawn you."

JEREMIAH 31:3 NKJV

Holy brothers, who share in the heavenly
calling, fix your thoughts on Jesus, the apostle
and high priest whom we confess.

HEBREWS 3:1

I am continually with You; You
hold me by my right hand.

PSALM 73:23 NKJV

DELIGHTFUL LORD,

I love listening to the song that You continually sing to me: *"I take great delight in you; I renew you by My Love; I shout for Joy over you."* The voices of this world are a cacophony of chaos, pulling me this way and that—especially in the weeks leading up to Christmas. Help me not to listen to those voices but to challenge them with Your Word. Show me how to take breaks from the noise of the world—finding a place to be still in Your Presence so I can hear Your voice.

I believe there is immense hidden treasure to be found through listening to You. You are always pouring out blessings upon me, but some of Your richest blessings have to be actively sought. I rejoice when You reveal Yourself to me—through Your Word, Your people, and the wonders of creation.

Having a seeking heart opens me up to receive more of You. The Bible gives me clear instructions: *Keep on asking and it will be given to you; keep on seeking and you will find; keep on knocking and the door will be opened to you.*

IN YOUR GENEROUS NAME, JESUS, AMEN

Let Me fill you
with My Love, Joy,
and Peace. These
are Glory-gifts,
flowing from My
living Presence.

The Lᴏʀᴅ your God is in your midst; he is a warrior who can deliver. He takes great delight in you; he renews you by his love; he shouts for joy over you."

ZᴇᴘʜᴀɴIᴀʜ 3:17 ɴᴇᴛ

While [Peter] was still speaking, a bright cloud overshadowed them, and behold, a voice out of the cloud said, "This is My beloved Son, with whom I am well pleased; listen to Him!"

MᴀᴛᴛHEW 17:5 ɴᴀsʙ

"Ask and keep on asking and it will be given to you; seek and keep on seeking and you will find; knock and keep on knocking and the door will be opened to you."

MᴀᴛᴛHEW 7:7 ᴀᴍᴘ

Restful Lord Jesus,

I come to You seeking to find rest in Your Presence. As I relax with You, Lord, I can enjoy Your Peace during this exciting, hectic season. *How precious it is, Lord, to realize that You are thinking about me constantly!* I long to be increasingly mindful of You. You've been teaching me that awareness of Your Presence can *give me rest* even when I'm very busy. An inner peacefulness flows out of remembering that *You are with me always.* This remembrance permeates my heart, mind, and spirit—filling me with Joy.

I confess that sometimes I get so focused on the problems I see and the predictions I hear that my joy gets buried under layers of worry and fear. When this happens, I need to bring my concerns to You—talking with You about each one, seeking Your help and guidance, asking You to remove those worry-layers. As I entrust My concerns into Your care and keeping, Joy begins to emerge again. I've learned that the most effective way for me to nurture this gladness is speaking and singing praises to You—*the King of Glory*!

In Your praiseworthy Name, amen

I, your Lord and
Savior, am alive
within you. Learn to
tune in to My living
Presence by seeking
Me in silence.

How precious it is, Lord, to realize that you
are thinking about me constantly! I can't even
count how many times a day your thoughts
turn toward me. And when I waken in the
morning, you are still thinking of me!

PSALM 139:17 TLB

"Surely I am with you always, to
the very end of the age."

MATTHEW 28:20

Lift up your heads, O you gates! And
be lifted up, you everlasting doors! And
the King of glory shall come in.

PSALM 24:7 NKJV

PRECIOUS JESUS,

During this Advent season, I am waiting for You with hope in my heart. Through reading Your Word, I've seen that waiting, trusting, and hoping are intricately connected—like golden strands woven together to form a strong chain. I think of *trusting* as the central strand because this attitude is taught so frequently throughout the Bible. Waiting and hoping embellish the central strand and strengthen the chain that connects me to You.

Waiting for You to work, with my eyes fixed on You, shows that I really do trust You. But if I simply mouth the words "I trust You" while anxiously trying to make things go my way, my words ring hollow.

Hoping is future-directed, connecting me to my glorious inheritance in heaven. However, as You have shown me, the benefits of hope fall fully on me in the present.

Because I belong to You, I don't just pass time in my waiting. I can wait expectantly, in hopeful trust. Please help me stay alert so I can pick up even the faintest glimmer of Your Presence.

IN YOUR TRUSTWORTHY NAME, AMEN

I care as much about
your tiny trust-steps
through daily life as
about your dramatic
leaps of faith. You may
think that no one notices,
but the One who is
always beside you sees
everything—and rejoices.

When I am afraid, I will put my trust in You. In God, whose word I praise, in God I have put my trust; I shall not be afraid. What can mere man do to me?

PSALM 56:3–4 NASB

Wait for the LORD; be strong, and let your heart take courage; wait for the LORD!

PSALM 27:14 ESV

Everyone who has this hope in Him purifies himself, just as He is pure.

1 JOHN 3:3 NKJV

Ever-present Jesus,

I rejoice that You are with me in all that I do—even in the most menial tasks. It's so comforting to know that You are always aware of me, concerned with every detail of my life. Nothing about me escapes Your notice—not even *the number of hairs on my head*. However, I confess that my awareness of Your Presence falters and flickers; as a result, my life experience often feels fragmented. When my focus is wide enough to include You in my thoughts, I feel safe and complete. But when my focus narrows so that problems and details and holiday to-do lists fill my mind, I lose sight of You. As a result, I feel empty and incomplete.

Lord, please teach me how to look steadily at You in all my moments and all my circumstances. Though this world is unstable and in flux, I can experience continuity by staying aware of Your steadfast Presence. Help me to *fix my eyes on what is unseen*—especially on *You*—even as the visible world parades before my eyes.

In Your faithful Name, amen

As you focus your thoughts on Me, be aware that I am fully attentive to you. I see you with a steady eye because My attention span is infinite. I know and understand you completely; My thoughts embrace you in everlasting Love.

"Are not two sparrows sold for a penny? Yet not one of them will fall to the ground apart from the will of your Father. And even the very hairs of your head are all numbered. So don't be afraid; you are worth more than many sparrows."

MATTHEW 10:29–31

By faith he left Egypt behind, not being afraid of the king's anger, for Moses persevered as one who sees Him who is invisible.

HEBREWS 11:27 HCSB

We fix our eyes not on what is seen, but on what is unseen. For what is seen is temporary, but what is unseen is eternal.

2 CORINTHIANS 4:18

BLESSED JESUS,

Help me learn to live above my circumstances. I realize this requires focused time with You, *the One who came to earth and has overcome the world.* Trouble and distress are woven into the very fabric of this perishing world. Only Your Life in me can empower me to face the endless flow of problems with *good cheer.*

As I relax in Your Presence—sitting quietly with You—You shine Peace into my troubled mind and heart. Little by little, through this time of focusing on You and Your Word, I am set free from earthly shackles and lifted above my circumstances. I gain Your perspective on my life—enabling me to distinguish between things that are important and things that are not. Moreover, resting in Your Presence blesses me with *Joy that no one will take away* from me.

IN YOUR JOYOUS NAME, AMEN

I meet you in the
stillness of your
soul. It is there that
I seek to commune
with you.

"These things I have spoken to you, that in Me you may have peace. In the world you will have tribulation; but be of good cheer, I have overcome the world."

JOHN 16:33 NKJV

Why are you in despair, O my soul? And why have you become disturbed within me? Hope in God, for I shall again praise Him for the help of His presence.

PSALM 42:5 NASB

"I will see you again and you will rejoice, and no one will take away your joy."

JOHN 16:22

BOUNTIFUL JESUS,

I give thanks to You, for You are good; Your Love endures forever. At this time of year when many are focused on gifts, I want to take time to think about the many blessings You provide. Thank You, Lord, for the gift of life—for every breath You give me. I'm grateful also for everyday provisions: food and water, shelter, clothing, family and friends. But the greatest gift I've received from You, my Savior, is everlasting Life!

As I consider all that You have done for me, I delight in who You are—the great *I Am*! You are one hundred percent good. There is not even a speck of darkness in You, *the Light of the world*! Moreover, Your Love is unending; it goes on and on throughout eternity.

Because I belong to You, I am never separated from Your loving Presence. I know that You are always near, so I don't need to worry about whether or not I sense Your Presence. Instead of focusing on my feelings, help me to simply trust that You are with me—and to *thank You for Your unfailing Love.*

IN YOUR BLESSED NAME, AMEN

I am the Gift that

continuously gives—

bounteously, with

no strings attached.

Give thanks to the Lord, for he is good;
his love endures forever.

PSALM 107:1

Jesus said to them, "Most assuredly, I say
to you, before Abraham was, I AM."

JOHN 8:58 NKJV

Again Jesus spoke to them, saying,
"I am the light of the world."

JOHN 8:12 ESV

Let them give thanks to the Lord for his unfailing
love and his wonderful deeds for men.

PSALM 107:8

MY GREAT GOD,

Only in *You* can I find lasting Joy. There are many sources of happiness in this world, and sometimes they spill over into Joy—especially when I share my pleasure with You. You shower so many blessings on my life! I want to take note of each one—responding to Your goodness with a glad, thankful heart. As I draw near to You with a grateful mindset, the Joy of Your Presence enhances the pleasure I receive from Your blessings.

On days when Joy seems a distant memory, I need to *seek Your Face* more than ever. Instead of letting circumstances or feelings weigh me down, I can encourage myself with biblical truth: *You are always with me; You hold me by my right hand. You guide me with Your counsel, and afterward You will take me into Glory.* I must hold on to these glorious truths with all my might as I make my way through the debris of this broken world. Help me remember that You Yourself are *the Truth*. You are also *the Way*, so it is wise to follow You. *The Light of Your Presence* is shining on me—illuminating the pathway before me.

IN YOUR BRIGHT NAME, JESUS, AMEN

Since I have

invested My very

Life in you, be

well assured that

I will also take

care of you.

I am always with you; you hold me by my
right hand. You guide me with your counsel,
and afterward you will take me into glory.

PSALM 73:23–24

Jesus said to him, I am the Way and the
Truth and the Life; no one comes to the
Father except by (through) Me.

JOHN 14:6 AMPC

Blessed are those who have learned to acclaim you,
who walk in the light of your presence, O LORD.

PSALM 89:15

My Savior-God,

Help me to rest deeply in You, forgetting about the worries of the world. May Your living Presence envelop me in Peace as I focus on You—*Immanuel*. I'm so thankful that You are *God with us*. I find comfort in Your eternal security, knowing that *You are the same yesterday, today, and forever.*

Sometimes I live too much on the surface of life—focusing on ever-changing phenomena. If I consistently live this way, I eventually reach the point where I echo the sentiment of Solomon: *"Meaningless! Meaningless! Everything is meaningless."*

I'm learning that the way to instill meaning into my days is to live in collaboration with You. I need to begin each day alone with You so I can experience the reality of Your Presence. As I spend time focusing on You and Your Word, I ask You to open up the way before me step by step. When I arise from this peaceful time of communion and begin my journey through the day, I'm aware that You go with me. I hold on to Your hand in deliberate dependence on You—and You smooth out the path before me. Thank You, Jesus!

In Your strong, dependable Name, Jesus, amen

Through
collaborating with
Me in all things,
you allow My Life
to merge with yours.
This is the secret of not
only joyful living but
also victorious living.

"The virgin will be with child and will give birth to a son, and they will call him Immanuel"—which means, "God with us."

MATTHEW 1:23

Jesus Christ is the same yesterday, today, and forever.

HEBREWS 13:8 NKJV

"Meaningless! Meaningless!" says the Teacher. ". . . Everything is meaningless."

ECCLESIASTES 1:2

WORTHY GOD,

The Bible assures me that *Your blessing is on those who trust in You, who put their confidence in You.* Please help me to trust You in the details of my life, just as Mary and Joseph did. I know that nothing is random in Your kingdom. *All things work together and are fitting into a plan for good—for those who love You and are called according to Your purpose.*

Instead of trying to figure everything out, I want to focus my energy on trusting and thanking You. I'm learning that nothing is wasted when I walk close to You. You've shown me that even my mistakes and sins can be recycled into something good—through Your transforming grace.

While I was still living in darkness, You began shining the Light of Your holy Presence into my sin-stained life. At the right time, *You lifted me out of the slimy pit, out of the mud and mire. You set my feet on a rock and gave me a firm place to stand.*

Thank You for calling me out of darkness into Your marvelous Light. Because of all You have done, I'm convinced that You can be trusted in every facet of my life!

IN YOUR SPLENDID NAME, JESUS, AMEN

I am taking care of
you. Trust Me at all
times. Trust Me in
all circumstances.

"My blessing is on those people who trust in me, who put their confidence in me."

JEREMIAH 17:7 NET

We are assured and know that [God being a partner in their labor] all things work together and are [fitting into a plan] for good to and for those who love God and are called according to [His] design and purpose.

ROMANS 8:28 AMPC

He lifted me out of the slimy pit, out of the mud and mire; he set my feet on a rock and gave me a firm place to stand.

PSALM 40:2

FAITHFUL GOD,

Help me *hold unswervingly to the hope I profess*, trusting that *You are faithful*. Sometimes—especially when many things are going wrong—all I can do is hold on to You. I would love to be able to sort things out in my mind and find the way forward, but often this is impossible. At such times, what I really need to do is *seek Your Face* and *profess my hope*.

To profess hope is to affirm it openly. My words matter—not only to other people but also to me. Speaking negatively discourages me as well as the people around me. But when my words affirm my hope and trust in You, I gain confidence that You will show me the way to proceed.

The basis of my confidence is that *You are faithful*. Moreover, You have promised *You will not let me be tempted beyond my ability to endure*. Sometimes *the way of escape* You provide comes through my own words, such as: "I trust You, Jesus; You are my hope." This affirmation keeps me holding on to You as my hope—unswervingly and trustingly.

IN YOUR hope-filled NAME, JESUS, AMEN

Do not fear your

weakness, for it is

the stage on which

My Power and

My Glory perform

most brilliantly.

Let us hold unswervingly to the hope we profess, for he who promised is faithful.

HEBREWS 10:23

◦◦◦

Hear, O LORD, when I cry with my voice! Have mercy also upon me, and answer me. When You said, "Seek My face," My heart said to You, "Your face, LORD, I will seek."

PSALM 27:7–8 NKJV

◦◦◦

No temptation has overtaken you that is not common to man. God is faithful, and he will not let you be tempted beyond your ability, but with the temptation he will also provide the way of escape, that you may be able to endure it.

1 CORINTHIANS 10:13 ESV

PEACEFUL SAVIOR,

Sometimes I feel lonely during the holidays. May Your Peace protect my mind and heart. Help me to *rejoice in You always*, remembering that *You are near*. As I spend time with You, *presenting my requests to You with thanksgiving*, You bless me with *Peace that transcends all understanding*. This is how You *guard my heart and my mind*. It's a collaborative, You-and-I together effort. I'm grateful that I never face anything alone!

Because I belong to You, aloneness is just an illusion—but it's a dangerous one that can lead to depression or self-pity. The devil and his underlings work hard to cloud my awareness of Your Presence. So it's crucial for me to recognize and resist their attacks. I can fight back with Your powerful Word, which is *living and active*—reading it, pondering it, memorizing it, speaking it out loud.

Even when I'm feeling alone, I can talk freely with You, trusting that *You are with me always*. I've discovered that the longer I talk with You, the more aware of Your nearness I become. And this awareness of Your Presence with me fills my heart and mind with Your Peace.

IN YOUR BELOVED NAME, JESUS, AMEN

When you feel far
from Me, whisper
My Name. This
simple act, done
in childlike faith,
opens your heart
to My Presence.

Rejoice in the Lord always. I will say it again: Rejoice! . . . The Lord is near. Do not be anxious about anything, but in everything, by prayer and petition, with thanksgiving, present your requests to God. And the peace of God, which transcends all understanding, will guard your hearts and your minds in Christ Jesus.

PHILIPPIANS 4:4–7

The word of God is living and active and sharper than any two-edged sword, and piercing as far as the division of soul and spirit, of both joints and marrow, and able to judge the thoughts and intentions of the heart.

HEBREWS 4:12 NASB

"Surely I am with you always, to the very end of the age."

MATTHEW 28:20

MERCIFUL LORD JESUS,

I come to You, asking You to prepare my heart for the celebration of Your birth. Christmas is the time to exult in Your miraculous incarnation, when You—*the Word—became flesh and made Your dwelling among us.* You identified with mankind to the ultimate extent: becoming a Man and taking up residence in our world. I don't want to let the familiarity of this astonishing miracle diminish its effect on me. You are the Gift above all gifts, and I *rejoice in You!*

A delightful way of opening up my heart to You is to spend time pondering the wonders of Your entrance into human history. I want to view these events from the perspective of *shepherds living out in the fields* near Bethlehem, *keeping watch over their flocks at night.* They witnessed first one angel and then *a great company of the heavenly host* lighting up the sky, proclaiming: *"Glory to God in the highest, and on earth Peace to those on whom His favor rests."*

Help me to gaze at the Glory of Your birth, just as the shepherds did, and respond with childlike wonder.

IN YOUR MARVELOUS, WONDROUS NAME, AMEN

Praise and worship are the best responses to the wonder of My Being. Sing praises to My holy Name!

"The voice of one crying in the wilderness: Prepare the way of the LORD; make His paths straight.'"

MARK 1:3 NKJV

❧

The Word became flesh and made his dwelling among us. We have seen his glory, the glory of the One and Only, who came from the Father, full of grace and truth.

JOHN 1:14

❧

There were shepherds living out in the fields nearby, keeping watch over their flocks at night. . . . Suddenly a great company of the heavenly host appeared with the angel, praising God and saying, "Glory to God in the highest, and on earth peace to men on whom his favor rests."

LUKE 2:8, 13–14

BRILLIANT JESUS,

You are the Light of the world! One way I like to celebrate Advent is by illuminating my home with candles and a lit-up tree. This is a way of symbolizing Your coming into our world—eternal Light breaking through the darkness and opening up the way to heaven. I'm grateful that nothing can reverse Your glorious plan of salvation. You've promised that all who trust You as Savior are adopted into Your royal family, to live with You forever!

Your Light shines on in the darkness, for the darkness has never overpowered it. No matter how much evil and unbelief I see in this dark world, You continue to shine brightly. So it's crucial for me to look toward the Light as much as possible—*fixing my eyes on You.* By making good thought-choices, I can "see" You as I journey through my days. Please help me to persevere in this delightful discipline of keeping my eyes on You. I find hope in these wonderful words that You spoke: *"Whoever follows Me will never walk in darkness, but will have the Light of Life."*

IN YOUR BRIGHT, RADIANT NAME, AMEN

Rejoice in all
that I have
done for you,
and My Light
will shine
through you
into the world.

When Jesus spoke again to the people, he said, "I am the light of the world. Whoever follows me will never walk in darkness, but will have the light of life."

JOHN 8:12

The Light shines on in the darkness, and the darkness did not understand it or overpower it.

JOHN 1:5 AMP

Let us fix our eyes on Jesus, the author and perfecter of our faith.

HEBREWS 12:2

GLORIOUS GOD,

Your Word assures me that *all those who wait for You are blessed*. Advent is a season of waiting—of waiting in hope. Waiting patiently does not come easily to me, but I know it is worth the effort. I like to plan ahead, make definitive decisions, and make things *happen*. There is a time for that, but this seems to be a time for waiting—sitting in Your Presence, seeking to trust You with my whole being. Though this discipline is certainly challenging for me, it is also quite delightful. Moreover, it brings a wealth of blessings.

Many of the good things You offer me reside in the future. While I spend time resting in Your Presence, You're preparing me for those not-yet blessings. Because they're veiled in the mystery of the future, I cannot see them clearly. Other blessings are for the present. I've found that the very process of waiting for You is highly beneficial. It keeps my soul on tiptoe as I look up to You in hope—acknowledging that You're in control and You are good. When I'm struggling to understand why I have to wait so long, please help me change my focus from *relying on my understanding* to *trusting You with all my heart*.

IN YOUR HOPE-FILLED NAME, JESUS, AMEN

Look to Me,
refreshing
yourself in My
Presence, and
your steps
will be steady
and sure.

The LORD longs to be gracious to you;
he rises to show you compassion. . . .
Blessed are all who wait for him!

ISAIAH 30:18

Let the morning bring me word of your unfailing
love, for I have put my trust in you. Show me the
way I should go, for to you I lift up my soul.

PSALM 143:8

Trust in the LORD with all your heart, and
do not rely on your own understanding.

PROVERBS 3:5 HCSB

PRINCE OF PEACE,

I come to You, feeling weary and burdened. As I take a break from the demands of this season, I want to spend time resting in Your Presence. I need Your Peace continually, just as I need *You* each moment.

When things are going smoothly in my life, it's easy to forget how dependent on You I really am. Then, when I encounter bumps in the road, I tend to become anxious and upset. Eventually, this revives my awareness of my need for You, and I return to You—seeking Your Peace. I'm thankful that You give me this glorious gift, but it's hard for me to receive it until I calm down. How much better it would be to stay close to You at all times!

Please help me remember that You, my Prince, are *Mighty God*! *All authority in heaven and on earth has been given to You.* Whenever I'm experiencing hard times, I can come to You and tell You my troubles. But I need to come humbly, acknowledging how great and wise You are. Rather than shaking my fist at You or insisting that You do things my way, I can pray these wonderful words of David: *"I trust in You, O Lord; I say, 'You are my God.' My times are in Your hands."*

IN YOUR MAJESTIC NAME, JESUS, AMEN

I designed you

to dwell in

Peace all day,

every day.

Draw near

to Me; receive

My Peace.

To us a Child is born, to us a Son is given; . . . and His name shall be called Wonderful Counselor, Mighty God, Everlasting Father . . . , Prince of Peace.

ISAIAH 9:6 AMPC

Jesus came to them and said, "All authority in heaven and on earth has been given to me."

MATTHEW 28:18

I trust in you, O LORD; I say, "You are my God." My times are in your hands.

PSALM 31:14–15

CHERISHED JESUS,

You are *the Joy that no one can take away from me*. As I rest in Your Presence, I savor the wonders of this glorious gift. I rejoice that this blessing is mine forever—*You* are mine for all eternity!

Many things in this world can bring me pleasure for a while, but they are all passing away due to death and decay. In *You* I have a matchless Treasure—Joy in the One who *is the same yesterday and today and forever*. No one can rob me of this pleasure because You are faithful and unchanging.

I realize that whenever I'm feeling joyless, the problem is not in the source of Joy (You) but in the receiver (me). Sometimes I get so focused on other things—difficulties and distractions in my life—that I neglect my relationship with You. Help me remember to put You first in my life, relating to You continually as my *First Love*. And please increase my moment-by-moment receptivity to Your Presence. As I spend time *delighting myself in You,* I receive Joy in full measure!

IN YOUR JOYOUS NAME, AMEN

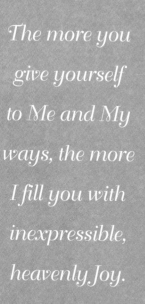

*The more you
give yourself
to Me and My
ways, the more
I fill you with
inexpressible,
heavenly Joy.*

"I will see you again and you will rejoice,
and no one will take away your joy."

JOHN 16:22

Jesus Christ is the same yesterday
and today and forever.

HEBREWS 13:8 ESV

Delight yourself in the LORD and he will
give you the desires of your heart.

PSALM 37:4

GENEROUS GOD,

You are a God of both intricate detail and overflowing abundance. When I entrust the details of my life to You, I'm often surprised by how thoroughly You answer my petitions. The biblical instruction to *pray continually* helps me feel free to bring You all my requests. And I've found that the more I pray—with a hopeful, watchful attitude—the more answers I receive. Best of all, my faith is strengthened as I see how precisely You respond to my specific prayers.

I rejoice that You are infinite in all Your ways! Because *abundance* is at the very heart of who You are, I don't need to fear that You will run out of resources. I can come to You in joyful expectation of receiving all I need—and sometimes much more!

I'm so grateful for the bountiful blessings You shower on me! Even the hardships in my life can be viewed as Your blessings—they train me in perseverance, transforming me and preparing me for heaven. Like a child receiving gifts on Christmas morning, I come to You with open hands and heart, ready to receive all that You have for me.

IN YOUR GREAT NAME, JESUS, AMEN

Nurture well your trust
in Me as Savior, Lord,
and Friend. I have held
back nothing in My
provision for you.

Pray continually.

1 THESSALONIANS 5:17

How priceless is your unfailing love! Both high and
low among men find refuge in the shadow of your
wings. They feast on the abundance of your house;
you give them drink from your river of delights.

PSALM 36:7–8

I will abundantly bless her provisions;
I will satisfy her poor with bread.

PSALM 132:15 ESV

EXALTED JESUS,

You are *the Light from on high that dawns upon us—to give Light to those who sit in darkness.* At Christmastime we're supposed to be joyful, but sometimes my circumstances are so difficult and confusing that I feel as if I'm surrounded by darkness. My mind offers up various solutions to my problems, but I've already tried them—without success. So I fret and wonder what to do next, feeling powerless and frustrated. At times like this, I need to look up and see Your Light shining upon me. As I gaze at You in childlike trust, I find hope and rest in Your Presence.

Your Word teaches me to *cease striving and know that You are God.* Please help me to set aside my problem-solving efforts and relax with You—remembering that You are the Prince of Peace. I find it soothing to breathe in Your peaceful Presence with each breath I take. The more of You I absorb, the calmer I become. After resting with You for a while, I'm ready to *pour out my heart* about my troubles—trusting You to show me the way I should go.

Lord, please *guide my feet into the way of Peace.*

IN YOUR WORTHY NAME, AMEN

Rest in the stillness
of My Presence
while I prepare you
for this day. Let
the radiance of My
Glory shine upon
you as you wait on
Me in confident trust.

Because of and through the heart of tender mercy and loving-kindness of our God, a Light from on high will dawn upon us and visit [us] to shine upon and give light to those who sit in darkness and in the shadow of death, to direct and guide our feet in a straight line into the way of peace.

LUKE 1:78–79 AMPC

"Cease striving and know that I am God; I will be exalted among the nations, I will be exalted in the earth."

PSALM 46:10 NASB

Trust in him at all times, O people; pour out your hearts to him, for God is our refuge.

PSALM 62:8

Powerful Savior,

You tell me in Your Word that *You are able to do immeasurably more than all I ask or imagine.* So I come to You with positive expectations, knowing there is no limit to what You can accomplish!

I confess, though, that I sometimes feel discouraged because so many of my long-term prayers are still unanswered. Please help me to wait patiently and with great hope—trusting You in the midst of uncertainty. You have promised that *those who wait for You will gain new strength*, and I definitely need more strength.

Instead of letting difficulties draw me into worry, I'm trying to view them as setting the scene for Your glorious intervention. You've shown me that the more extreme my circumstances, the more likely I am to see Your *Power and Glory* at work in the situation. Lord, I long to live with my eyes and my mind fully open—beholding all that You are doing in my life!

In Your holy Name, Jesus, amen

Every moment is alive
with My glorious
Presence, to those whose
hearts are intimately
connected with Mine.
As you give yourself
more and more to a life
of constant communion
with Me, you will find
that you simply have
no time for worry.

Now to him who is able to do immeasurably more than all we ask or imagine, according to his power that is at work within us, to him be glory in the church and in Christ Jesus throughout all generations, for ever and ever! Amen.

EPHESIANS 3:20–21

Though youths grow weary and tired, and vigorous young men stumble badly, yet those who wait for the LORD will gain new strength; they will mount up with wings like eagles, they will run and not get tired, they will walk and not become weary.

ISAIAH 40:30–31 NASB

I have looked upon you in the sanctuary, beholding your power and glory.

PSALM 63:2 ESV

PRECIOUS LORD JESUS,

You are *Immanuel, God with us*—and You are enough! When things in my life are flowing smoothly, it's easy for me to trust in Your sufficiency. But when I encounter rough patches—one after another after another—I sometimes feel as if Your provision is inadequate. At times like this, my mind tends to go into high gear, obsessing about ways to make things better. I've come to realize that problem solving can turn into an addiction. There are times when my mind spins with so many plans and possibilities that I become confused and exhausted.

Instead of being overly focused on problems, I need to remember that *You are with me always*, taking care of me. Help me to *rejoice in You* and proclaim Your sufficiency even during my most difficult times. This is a supernatural response, and I must rely on Your Spirit to empower me. I also have to discipline myself to make wise choices—day by day and moment by moment. Lord, I choose to *be joyful in You, my Savior*, for You are indeed enough!

IN YOUR ALL-SUFFICIENT NAME, AMEN

If you could only see

how close I am to you

and how constantly I

work on your behalf,

you would never

again doubt that

I am wonderfully

caring for you.

"She will give birth to a son, and you are to give him the name Jesus, because he will save his people from their sins." All this took place to fulfill what the Lord had said through the prophet: "The virgin will be with child and will give birth to a son, and they will call him Immanuel"—which means, "God with us."

MATTHEW 1:21–23

❧

"Behold, I am with you always, to the end of the age."

MATTHEW 28:20 ESV

❧

Though the fig tree does not bud and there are no grapes on the vines, though the olive crop fails and the fields produce no food, though there are no sheep in the pen and no cattle in the stalls, yet I will rejoice in the LORD, I will be joyful in God my Savior.

HABAKKUK 3:17–18

My great God,

I'm grateful that *Your compassions never fail; they are new every morning*. So I can begin each day confidently, knowing that Your vast reservoir of blessings is full to the brim! This knowledge helps me wait for You, entrusting my long-unanswered prayers into Your care and keeping. I trust that not even one of my petitions has slipped past You unnoticed. As I wait in Your Presence, help me to drink deeply from Your fountain of limitless Love and unfailing compassion. These divine provisions are freely available to me—and essential for my spiritual health.

Although many of my prayers are not yet answered, I find hope in *Your great faithfulness*. You keep *all* Your promises—in Your perfect way and Your perfect timing. You have promised to give me Peace that can displace the trouble and fear in my heart. Thank You, Jesus, for coming into the world to bring Peace to *those with whom You are pleased*.

If I become weary of waiting, please remind me that You also wait—*so that You may be gracious to me and have mercy on me*. You hold back until I am ready to receive the things You have lovingly prepared for me. As I spend time in Your Presence, I rejoice in the promise that *all those who wait for You are blessed*.

In Your gracious Name, Jesus, amen

As you rest in

My Presence,

focusing on Me,

I quietly build

bonds of trust

between us.

Because of the LORD's great love we are not consumed, for his compassions never fail. They are new every morning; great is your faithfulness.

LAMENTATIONS 3:22–23

"Peace I leave with you; my peace I give you. . . . Do not let your hearts be troubled and do not be afraid."

JOHN 14:27

"Glory to God in the highest, and on earth peace among those with whom he is pleased!"

LUKE 2:14 ESV

The LORD will wait, that He may be gracious to you; and therefore He will be exalted, that He may have mercy on you. . . . Blessed are all those who wait for Him.

ISAIAH 30:18 NKJV ,

Beloved Jesus,

As I read Your Word this December morning, my mind and heart are quiet, and I can hear You inviting me to *draw near*. I delight in Your glorious invitation, proclaimed in holy whispers: *"Come to Me. Come to Me. Come to Me."* Drawing near to You requires no great effort on my part; it's more like surrendering to You and ceasing to resist the magnetic pull of Your Love.

Help me, *through Your Spirit,* to open myself more fully to Your loving Presence *so that I may be filled to the measure of all Your fullness.* I yearn to *have power to grasp how wide and long and high and deep is Your Love for me— and to know this Love that surpasses knowledge.* This vast ocean of Love cannot be measured or explained, but it can be experienced.

In Your amazing Name, amen

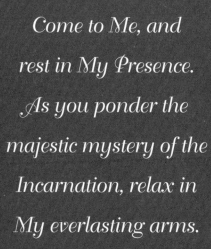

*Come to Me, and
rest in My Presence.
As you ponder the
majestic mystery of the
Incarnation, relax in
My everlasting arms.*

Draw near to God and He will draw near to you.

JAMES 4:8 NASB

⚬

"Everyone the Father gives Me will come to Me, and
the one who comes to Me I will never cast out."

JOHN 6:37 HCSB

⚬

I pray that out of his glorious riches he may strengthen
you with power through his Spirit in your inner being, so
that Christ may dwell in your hearts through faith. And I
pray that you . . . may have power . . . to grasp how wide
and long and high and deep is the love of Christ, and
to know this love that surpasses knowledge—that you
may be filled to the measure of all the fullness of God.

EPHESIANS 3:16–19

Peace on Earth

MAGNIFICENT SAVIOR,

The Joy I have in You is independent of my circumstances. I am never separated from You, and *in Your Presence there is fullness of Joy*! As I go along today's pathway, preparing for Christmas, I'll search for signs of Your unseen yet ever-so-real Presence. Sometimes You communicate with me in grand, unmistakable ways—"Coincidences" that are clearly the work of Your hands. At other times I get more subtle glimpses of You. These are often so personal and intimate that other people wouldn't even notice them. Yet these subtle signs bring me profound Joy.

The more attentive I am, the more I can find You in the details of my day. So please help me stay alert—being on the lookout for delightful displays of Your Presence.

I want to fill my mind and heart with Scripture, where You reveal Yourself most clearly. As Your promises permeate my thinking, they keep me close to You. I love to hear You speaking to me through Your Word: *"Listen to My voice. I know you, and you follow Me. I give you eternal Life, and no one can snatch you out of My hand."*

IN YOUR INVINCIBLE NAME, JESUS, AMEN

Let Scripture saturate your mind and heart, and you will walk steadily along the path of Life. Even though you don't know what will happen tomorrow, you can be absolutely sure of your ultimate destination.

You make known to me the path of life; in
your presence there is fullness of joy; at your
right hand are pleasures forevermore.

PSALM 16:11 ESV

"You will seek Me and find Me, when you
search for Me with all your heart."

JEREMIAH 29:13 NKJV

"My sheep listen to my voice; I know them, and they
follow me. I give them eternal life, and they shall never
perish; no one can snatch them out of my hand."

JOHN 10:27–28

Mighty Jesus,

All things are possible with You! These powerful words from Scripture light up my mind and encourage my heart. You are training me to *live by faith, not by sight.* So I refuse to be intimidated by the way things look at this moment.

I'm thankful for the sense of sight, a spectacular gift from You. But with dazzling lights and decorations all around, it's easy for me to be so mesmerized by the visual stimulation that You fade into the background of my mind. Help me instead to focus primarily on *You*—trusting in Your promises and trying to see things from Your perspective.

Teach me how to grow closer to You, Lord Jesus. I delight in knowing You as my Savior and Friend, but I want to relate to You also as Almighty God. When You lived as a Man in this world, *Your miraculous signs revealed Your Glory*. I know that You continue to do miracles according to Your will and purposes. Please train me to align my will with Yours and to *watch in hope for You* to work.

In Your powerful Name, amen

Relax in the knowledge
that the One who
controls your life is
totally trustworthy. Come
to Me with confident
expectation. There is
nothing you need that
I cannot provide.

Jesus looked at them and said, "With man
it is impossible, but not with God. For
all things are possible with God."

MARK 10:27 ESV

We live by faith, not by sight.

2 CORINTHIANS 5:7

This, the first of his miraculous signs, Jesus
performed at Cana of Galilee. He thus revealed
his glory, and his disciples put their faith in him.

JOHN 2:11

But as for me, I watch in hope for the Lord, I
wait for God my Savior; my God will hear me.

MICAH 7:7

IMMANUEL,

Stillness is increasingly hard to come by in this restless, agitated world. With Christmas fast approaching, I really have to fight to carve out time for You. Distractions come at me from all sides when I try to sit quietly with You. But having an intimate connection with You is worth fighting for, so I won't give up!

Please help me in my quest to set aside uninterrupted time to spend with You—focusing on You and Your Word. I'm so grateful that You are Immanuel—God with us. As I relax in Your peaceful Presence, letting my concerns slip away, I can hear You whispering to me: *"Be still, and know that I am God."*

The longer I gaze at You, the more I can rejoice in Your majestic splendors—and trust in Your sovereign control. *You are my Refuge, though the earth give way and the mountains fall into the heart of the sea.* There is transcendent stability in Your Presence, Lord. As I ponder the vastness of Your Power and Glory, my perspective changes and my problems look smaller. I know *I will have trouble in this world*, but I'm encouraged by Your assurance that *You have overcome the world.*

IN YOUR CONQUERING NAME, JESUS, AMEN

I am pleased with your
desire to create a quiet space
where you and I can meet.
Don't be discouraged by
the difficulty of achieving
this goal. I monitor all
your efforts and am
blessed by each of your
attempts to seek My Face.

"Be still, and know that I am God; I will be exalted among the nations, I will be exalted in the earth!"

PSALM 46:10 NKJV

God is our refuge and strength, an ever-present help in trouble. Therefore we will not fear, though the earth give way and the mountains fall into the heart of the sea.

PSALM 46:1–2

"I have told you these things, so that in me you may have peace. In this world you will have trouble. But take heart! I have overcome the world."

JOHN 16:33

MY GREAT GOD,

I love hearing You speak through Your Word: *"I am making everything new!"* This is the opposite of what is happening in my world of death and decay. I realize that every day I live means one less day remaining in my lifespan on earth. But because I belong to You, Jesus, this thought doesn't trouble me. At the end of each day, I'm mindful of being one step closer to heaven.

The world is in such a desperately fallen condition that Your promise to *make everything new* is my only hope. Help me not to get discouraged when my efforts to improve matters are unsuccessful. I must keep in mind that all my efforts are tainted by the brokenness around me and within me. I won't stop trying to do my best—in dependence on You—but I know that this world needs much more than a tune-up or repairs. It needs to be made completely new! And this is absolutely guaranteed to happen at the end of time, for *Your words are trustworthy and true.*

I have good reason to rejoice this Christmas because You have promised to renew all things—including me—making everything gloriously perfect!

IN YOUR TRIUMPHANT NAME, JESUS, AMEN

Do not fear what this day, or any day, may bring your way. Concentrate on trusting Me and on doing what needs to be done. Relax in My sovereignty, remembering that I go before you, as well as with you, into each day.

He who was seated on the throne said, "I am making everything new!" Then he said, "Write this down, for these words are trustworthy and true."

REVELATION 21:5

To me, to live is Christ, and to die is gain.

PHILIPPIANS 1:21 NKJV

We know that the whole creation has been groaning as in the pains of childbirth right up to the present time. Not only so, but we ourselves, who have the firstfruits of the Spirit, groan inwardly as we wait eagerly for our adoption as sons, the redemption of our bodies.

ROMANS 8:22–23

CHERISHED JESUS,

You are my Joy! These four words light up my life when I think them, whisper them, or speak them out loud. Since You are always with me, *the Joy of Your Presence* is continually available to me. I can open my heart to Your Presence by affirming my trust in You, my love for You. Your Light shines upon me and within me as I rejoice in You, my Savior. I delight in thinking about all that You are to me and all You have done for me.

When I became Your follower, You empowered me to rise above the circumstances in my life. You filled me with Your Spirit, and this Holy Helper has limitless Power. Moreover, You promised that *You will come back and take me to be with You so that I may be where You are*—forever!

Whenever my world looks dark, focusing on You—*the Light of the world*—brightens my perspective. As I relax in Your Presence, I can almost hear You whispering, "Beloved, I am Your Joy."

IN YOUR BEAUTIFUL NAME, AMEN

I want you to
reflect My joyous
Light by living
in increasing
intimacy with Me.

Surely you have granted him eternal
blessings and made him glad with
the joy of your presence.

PSALM 21:6

"If I go and prepare a place for you, I
will come back and take you to be with
me that you also may be where I am."

JOHN 14:3

When Jesus spoke again to the people,
he said, "I am the light of the world.
Whoever follows me will never walk in
darkness, but will have the light of life."

JOHN 8:12

Eternal God,

In the beginning was the Word, and the Word was with God, and the Word was God. You are *the Word that became flesh*—You have always been, and You will always be. Help me not to lose sight of Your divinity as I celebrate Your birth.

I'm so thankful that You grew up to become the Man-Savior who is God Almighty! If You were not God, Your sacrificial life and death would have been insufficient to provide salvation. I rejoice that You, who entered the world as a helpless infant, are the very same One who brought the world into existence.

Though You were rich, for my sake You became poor, so that through Your poverty I might become rich. No Christmas present could ever compare with the infinite treasure I have in You! Because of You, my sins have been removed *as far as the east is from the west*—freeing me from all condemnation. You have gifted me with unimaginably glorious Life that will never end! Thank You, Lord, for this breathtaking Gift; I embrace it joyously and gratefully.

In Your supreme Name, Jesus, amen

As you celebrate
the wonder of
My birth in
Bethlehem,
celebrate also
your rebirth
into eternal life.

In the beginning was the Word, and the Word was with God, and the Word was God. . . . The Word became flesh and made his dwelling among us. We have seen his glory, the glory of the One and Only, who came from the Father, full of grace and truth.

JOHN 1:1, 14

You know the grace of our Lord Jesus Christ, that though He was rich, yet for your sake He became poor, so that you through His poverty might become rich.

2 CORINTHIANS 8:9 NASB

As far as the east is from the west, so far has He removed our transgressions from us.

PSALM 103:12 NKJV

Treasured Jesus,

Help me remember that challenging circumstances come and go, but *You are continually with me*. The constancy of Your Presence is a glorious treasure that's immeasurably better than any Christmas gift!

It comforts me to know that You are writing the storyline of my life—through good times *and* hard times. You can see the big picture: from before my birth to beyond the grave. And You know exactly what I will be like when heaven becomes my forever-home. Moreover, You're constantly at work in me—changing me into the person You designed me to be. Your Word assures me that I am royalty in Your kingdom.

One of my favorite ways to draw near You is to lovingly speak Your Name. This simple prayer expresses my trust that You are indeed with me and You're taking care of me. You, *the God of hope, fill me with all Joy and Peace as I trust in You*.

No matter how heavy my burdens are, the reality of Your Presence with me outweighs all my difficulties. When I wait quietly with You, I can hear You whisper: *"Come to Me, all you who are weary and burdened, and I will give you rest."*

In Your refreshing Name, amen

134

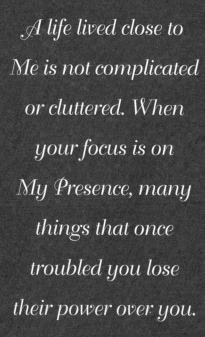

A life lived close to Me is not complicated or cluttered. When your focus is on My Presence, many things that once troubled you lose their power over you.

I am continually with You; You
hold me by my right hand.

PSALM 73:23 NKJV

May the God of hope fill you with all joy and peace
as you trust in him, so that you may overflow
with hope by the power of the Holy Spirit.

ROMANS 15:13

"Come to me, all you who are weary and
burdened, and I will give you rest."

MATTHEW 11:28

EVER-PRESENT JESUS,

I love to hear You whispering to me, *"I am with you. I am with you. I am with you."* It's as if heaven's bells are continually pealing with that promise of Your Presence. Sadly, some people never hear those glorious bells because their minds are earthbound and their hearts are closed to You. Others may hear the wondrous proclamations of Your Presence only once or twice in their lifetimes—in rare moments of seeking You above all else. You are my ever-present Shepherd, and I want to be a sheep who stays attentive to You—*listening to Your voice.*

Quietness is the classroom where You are teaching me to hear Your voice. I need a quiet place in order to calm my mind. I seem to be a slow learner, so please help me advance in this delightful discipline. Eventually, I hope to be able to carry the calmness with me wherever I go. Though I'm still a novice, sometimes I can hear those melodious bells when I step back into the bustle of life: *"I am with you. I am with you. I am with you."*

Immanuel, I rejoice in You!

IN YOUR DELIGHTFUL, CALMING NAME, AMEN

Seek My Face
continually throughout
this day. Let My
Presence bring order
to your thoughts,
infusing Peace into
your entire being.

"Fear not, for I am with you; be not dismayed, for I am
your God. I will strengthen you, yes, I will help you,
I will uphold you with My righteous right hand."

ISAIAH 41:10 NKJV

"You will call upon me and come and pray to me,
and I will listen to you. You will seek me and find
me when you seek me with all your heart."

JEREMIAH 29:12–13

"I am the good shepherd; I know my sheep and my sheep
know me. . . . My sheep listen to my voice; I know them,
and they follow me. I give them eternal life, and they shall
never perish; no one can snatch them out of my hand."

JOHN 10:14, 27–28

MAJESTIC JESUS,

Your unfailing Love is better than life itself! I'm grateful that there's no limit to Your Love—in quality, quantity, or duration. *How priceless is Your unfailing Love!* It is infinitely better than anything this world can offer, and it will never run out. This Love is so precious that it's worth losing everything else to secure it.

Though gaining Your Love is worth losing my life, this glorious gift greatly *enriches* my life. Your steadfast Love provides a firm foundation for me to build on. Knowing I'm perfectly, eternally loved improves my relationships with others and helps me grow into the person You designed me to be. Moreover, *grasping how wide and long and high and deep is Your Love* for me leads me into worship. *This* is where my intimacy with You grows by leaps and bounds—as I joyously celebrate Your magnificent Presence!

As Christmas Day approaches, my heart echoes the words of the psalmist: *Let everything that has breath praise the Lord.* I praise You, Lord!

IN YOUR PRAISEWORTHY NAME, AMEN

Take time to explore
the vast dimensions
of My Love. Allow
thankfulness to flow
freely from your
heart in response to
My glorious gift.

Your unfailing love is better than
life itself; how I praise you!

PSALM 63:3 NLT

How priceless is your unfailing love, O God!

PSALM 36:7

I pray that you, being rooted and established in
love, may have power . . . to grasp how wide and
long and high and deep is the love of Christ.

EPHESIANS 3:17–18

Let everything that has breath praise
the LORD. Praise the LORD!

PSALM 150:6 NKJV

IMMANUEL,

You are *God with us*—at all times. This promise from Your Word provides a solid foundation for my Joy. Sometimes I try to pin my pleasure to temporary things, but Your Presence with me is an eternal blessing. I rejoice that You, my Savior, have promised *You will never leave me.*

The nature of time can make it difficult for me to fully enjoy my life. On those days when everything is going well, my awareness that the ideal conditions are fleeting can dampen my enjoyment. Even the most delightful vacation must eventually come to an end. Seasons of life also come and go, despite my longing at times to stop the clock and keep things as they are.

I don't want to look down on the temporary pleasures You provide, but I *do* need to accept their limitations—their inability to quench the thirst of my soul. Please help me remember that my search for lasting Joy will fail unless I make *You* the ultimate goal of my quest. *In Your Presence there is fullness of Joy.*

IN YOUR JOYFUL NAME, JESUS, AMEN

In the intimacy of
My Presence you are
energized. No matter
where you are in the
world, you know you
belong when you
sense My nearness.

"Behold, the virgin shall be with child, and bear a Son, and they shall call His name Immanuel," which is translated, "God with us."

MATTHEW 1:23 NKJV

Be satisfied with what you have, for He Himself has said, I will never leave you or forsake you.

HEBREWS 13:5 HCSB

You will show me the path of life; in Your presence is fullness of joy; at Your right hand are pleasures forevermore.

PSALM 16:11 NKJV

Compassionate Jesus,

You came into the world as a Light so that no one who believes in You would stay in darkness. You didn't just *bring* Light into the world; You are *the Light that shines on in the darkness, for the darkness has never overpowered it.* Nothing can extinguish this illumination because You are infinite and all-powerful!

When I believed in You, I became a *child of Light.* Your brightness entered into my inner being, enabling me to see from Your perspective—things in the world *and* things in my heart. When Your Spirit illumines the contents of my heart and shows me things that are displeasing to You, help me to repent and walk in Your ways. This is the road to freedom.

Lord, I rejoice in my brightened perspective. *The god of this age has blinded the minds of unbelievers so that they cannot see the Light of the gospel of Your Glory.* But because I belong to You, I have *the Light of the knowledge of Your Glory* shining in my heart! Thank You, Jesus!

IN YOUR BRIGHT, ILLUMINATING NAME, AMEN

I rejoice when your mind turns toward Me. Guard your thoughts diligently; good thought-choices will keep you close to Me.

"I have come into the world as a light, so that no one who believes in me should stay in darkness."

JOHN 12:46

The Light shines on in the darkness, for the darkness has never overpowered it.

JOHN 1:5 AMPC

The god of this age has blinded the minds of unbelievers, so that they cannot see the light of the gospel of the glory of Christ, who is the image of God. . . . God . . . made his light shine in our hearts to give us the light of the knowledge of the glory of God in the face of Christ.

2 CORINTHIANS 4:4, 6

GLORIOUS JESUS,

As I wait attentively in Your Presence, *the Light of the knowledge of Your Glory* shines upon me. This radiant knowledge utterly transcends my understanding. Moreover, it transforms my entire being—renewing my mind, cleansing my heart, invigorating my body. Help me to open myself fully to Your glorious Presence!

I cannot imagine what You gave up when You came into our world as a baby. You set aside Your Glory so that You could identify with mankind—with me. You accepted the limitations of infancy under appalling conditions: born in a stable, with a feeding trough for Your crib. There was nothing glorious about the setting of Your birth, even though angels lit up the sky proclaiming "Glory!" to awestruck shepherds.

Sitting quietly with You, I experience the reverse of what You went through. *You became poor so that I might become rich.* As I draw nearer to You, heaven's vistas open up before me—granting me glimpses of Your Glory. O Lord, I sing hallelujahs to Your holy Name!

IN YOUR SACRED NAME, AMEN

I am the Creator of the entire universe, yet I choose to make My humble home in your heart. It is there where you know Me most intimately; it is there were I speak to you in holy whispers. Ask My Spirit to quiet your mind so that you can hear My still small voice within you. I am speaking to you continually: words of Life . . . Peace . . . Love.

God, who said, "Let light shine out of darkness," made his light shine in our hearts to give us the light of the knowledge of the glory of God in the face of Christ.

2 Corinthians 4:6

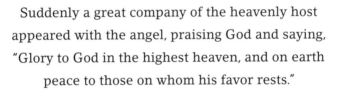

Suddenly a great company of the heavenly host appeared with the angel, praising God and saying, "Glory to God in the highest heaven, and on earth peace to those on whom his favor rests."

Luke 2:13–14

You know the grace of our Lord Jesus Christ, that though He was rich, yet for your sakes He became poor, that you through His poverty might become rich.

2 Corinthians 8:9 nkjv

Precious Lord Jesus,

When an angel announced Your birth to *shepherds living out in the fields* near Bethlehem, he told them: *"Do not be afraid. I bring you good tidings of great Joy."* This command to not be afraid is repeated frequently throughout the Bible. Thank You for providing this tender, merciful directive. You know how prone to fear I am, yet You do not condemn me for it. However, I do want to break free from my inclination to be fearful.

I've discovered that Joy is a powerful antidote to fear. And the greater the Joy, the more effective an antidote it is. The angel's announcement to the shepherds was one of *great* Joy! Help me never to lose sight of what amazingly good news the gospel is!

The moment I trusted You as my Savior, You forgave *all* my sins—past, present, and future. This glorious gift of grace ensures that my ultimate destination is heaven. Moreover, You gave me *Yourself*—the greatest treasure of all! You lavished Your Love on me and promised me Your Presence forever. As I ponder the angel's wondrous proclamation to the shepherds, I *rejoice in You*, my beloved Savior.

In Your magnificent Name, amen

I want you to come into
My Presence joyfully
and confidently. You
have nothing to fear,
for you wear My own
righteousness. Gaze into
My eyes, and you will see
no condemnation, only Love
and delight in the one I see.

Now there were in the same country shepherds living out in the fields, keeping watch over their flock by night. And behold, an angel of the Lord stood before them, and the glory of the Lord shone around them, and they were greatly afraid. Then the angel said to them, "Do not be afraid, for behold, I bring you good tidings of great joy which will be to all people."

LUKE 2:8–10 NKJV

By grace you have been saved through faith. And this is not your own doing; it is the gift of God.

EPHESIANS 2:8 ESV

Rejoice in the Lord always. I will say it again: Rejoice!

PHILIPPIANS 4:4

KING JESUS,

You are *King of kings and Lord of lords; You dwell in unapproachable Light*! I'm grateful that You are also my Shepherd, Companion, and Friend—the One who never lets go of my hand. I worship You in Your holy Majesty. And I draw near You to rest in Your loving Presence. I need You both as God and as Man. Only Your birth on that first, long-ago Christmas could meet all my needs.

Instead of trying to comprehend Your incarnation intellectually, I want to learn from the example of the wise men. They followed the leading of a spectacular star, then fell down in humble worship in Your Presence. Inspired by the magi, I long to respond to the wonder of Your holy birth with ardent adoration.

Please help me grow in my capacity to worship You as my Savior, Lord, and King. You held back nothing in Your amazing provision for me, and I rejoice in all that You are—all You have done!

You are *the Light from on high that dawns upon us, to direct and guide our feet into the way of Peace.*

IN YOUR MAJESTIC NAME, AMEN

*Let your life
become a praise
song to Me by
proclaiming
My glorious
presence in
the world.*

God will bring about [the appearing of our Lord Jesus Christ] in his own time—God, the blessed and only Ruler, the King of kings and Lord of lords, who alone is immortal and who lives in unapproachable light, whom no one has seen or can see. To him be honor and might forever. Amen.

1 TIMOTHY 6:15–16

When they saw the star, they rejoiced with exceedingly great joy. And when they had come into the house, they saw the young Child with Mary His mother, and fell down and worshiped Him.

MATTHEW 2:10–11 NKJV

A Light from on high will dawn upon us and visit [us] to shine upon and give light to those who sit in darkness and in the shadow of death, to direct and guide our feet in a straight line into the way of peace.

LUKE 1:78–79 AMPC

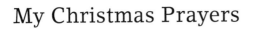

My Christmas Prayers

My Christmas Prayers

About the Author

Sarah Young, author of the bestselling 365-day devotionals *Jesus Calling* and *Jesus Listens*, has sold more than 40 million books worldwide. *Jesus Calling* has appeared on all major bestseller lists. Sarah's writings include *Jesus Calling, Jesus Listens, Jesus Always, Jesus Today, Jesus Lives, Dear Jesus, Jesus Calling for Little Ones, Jesus Calling Bible Storybook, Jesus Calling: 365 Devotions for Kids, Peace in His Presence*, and more, each encouraging readers in their journeys toward intimacy with Christ. Sarah and her husband were missionaries in Japan and Australia for many years. They currently live in the United States. Sarah enjoys praying daily for readers of all her books.

Connect with Sarah at:
Facebook.com/JesusCalling
Instagram.com/JesusCalling
Youtube.com/jesuscallingbook
Pinterest.com/Jesus_Calling
Twitter.com/Jesus_Calling
JesusCalling.com

Experience Peace
in His Presence

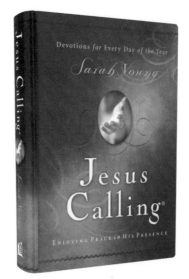

Written as if Jesus Himself is speaking directly
to you—words of encouragement, comfort,
and reassurance of His unending love.

Jesus Calling® is your yearlong guide to living a more
peaceful life, delivering His message of love every day.

"I AM THE GIFT that continuously gives—bounteously, with no strings attached. Unconditional Love is such a radical concept, that even My most devoted followers fail to grasp it fully. Absolutely nothing in heaven or on earth can cause Me to stop loving you."

—AN EXCERPT FROM *JESUS CALLING*

"Strong Savior,

Your Word assures me that You are both with me and for me. When I decide on a course of action that conforms to Your will, nothing can stop me. So I won't give up, even if I encounter multiple obstacles as I move toward my goal. I know there will be many ups and downs as I journey with You, but *with Your help* I can overcome any obstacle. I'm encouraged by the glorious truth that You, my *ever-present Help*, are omnipotent!"

—AN EXCERPT FROM *JESUS LISTENS*

When it feels like no one hears you . . . Jesus Listens!

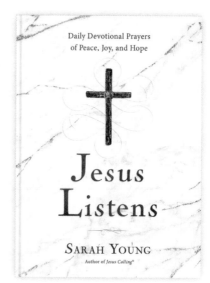

Daily Devotional Prayers of Peace, Joy, and Hope

Jesus Listens

SARAH YOUNG
Author of *Jesus Calling*

"I hope you will not only read these prayers but make them your own."
—Sarah Young

When life has you anxious and stressed, you can find peace and hope in Jesus. This 365-day devotional prayer book from the author of *Jesus Calling*® will give you the confidence to come to God in all circumstances with short, heartfelt prayers based on Scripture.

Invite the hope of Jesus and the joy of the nativity into little hearts

Celebrate Advent and Christmas with this read-aloud children's prayer book by Sarah Young, bestselling author of *Jesus Calling*. This board book (for ages 0–4) includes an Advent calendar of 25 prayers alongside a simple retelling of the Christmas story.